Designed to Decrease Aggressive Behavior on the Part of Students in the Classroom

Designed to Decrease Aggressive Behavior on the Part of Students in the Classroom

Classroom Behavior Management

A Ph.D. Dissertation

Dr. Roxanne Contee

To order additional copies of this book, contact:
Xlibris Corporation
1-888-795-4274
www.Xlibris.com
Orders@Xlibris.com
94463

Contents

Special Thanks and Acknowledgements

After a long endeavor in my efforts to publish my book on *"Classroom management and how to decrease behaviors in the classroom,"* the book is finally out. Therefore, I would like to take this opportunity to give thanks to all who supported me in this long journey. First and foremost, I must give praise, glory and honor to Jesus Christ, because without Him there would be no me. I love the lord Jesus Christ and I ask Him to continue working in me. I dedicate myself to Him because he helps me to produce the best for the glory of His name. To Him be all the glory and honor forever and ever more Amen. Secondly, I would like to thank my parents who raised me up with diligence and taught me to work hard and be positive in life. Without their support I would not have been able to make it this far. In fact this book is a special dedication to my parents who have always been loving and caring to me in all ways. Apart from bringing me into this wonderful world and raising me to be a successful person, my parents have remained my mentors in every aspect of life. Their advice and concern for me has often struck me with awe. I thank my mother and my father for their nurturing love for me. I promise to make them proud in every endeavor I take. This book is manifestation of the care and love I received from my parents. To my teachers, I would like to commend you for training me in every aspect, equipping me with knowledge and wisdom that enabled me to produce this book. I would not have known what to write in this book without your instruction. Finally I would like to thank my college professors for nurturing my talents and guiding me in every way so as to be successful in this endeavor. I thank them more since I shared with them my vision and none of them discouraged me. I am extremely grateful.

The book on *"Classroom management and how to decrease behaviors in the classroom,"* reflects my passion of teaching. I am naturally endowed with the love of teaching. Therefore, I chose this topic because of the passion for teaching. Furthermore, in my experiences in the field of teaching I have noted certain behaviors that I thought hinder the teaching process. Therefore, in order to complement my love for teaching, I decided to write a book on how to manage classroom affairs so as to be successful in teaching. This book is a guide to anyone who is in the teaching profession as well as those who endeavor to join the career. It is well equipped to provide the necessary assistance needed for the purposes of being successful in the teaching practice. As the title suggests, the book is about handling the classroom so as to minimize the behaviors that obstruct successful teaching. Some of these behaviors are learned and natural. However, a clear understanding of them will produce a better way of reducing their impact on teaching. My love and passion for teaching has often made me look at teaching in a critical perspective. My endeavor has always been to look for ways of improving teaching so as to be successful in the whole profession. Therefore, I chose the topic so as to nurture appropriate management skills among teachers as well as equipping them to help students learn better. I believe the book with go a long way in improving teaching and classroom management.

Chapter I:
Introduction or Problem Statement

Aggressive behavior in the classroom can take many dimensions, such as bullying, which in turn, can lead to poor school performance and absenteeism, and a host of other types of aggressive behavior are equally interrelated. Anyway, it is the intent of this author to provide a general introduction to this dissertation. Herein, this author shall briefly discuss what this author shall be attesting, as well as the statement of any hypothesis that this author shall be testing and reasons for choosing this topic, etc. It is the intent of this author to prove or disprove in this dissertation, which will largely be predicated upon, the hypothesis as identified by this author throughout this dissertation. To this extent, this author shall provide a plethora of foundational information vis-à-vis what this author is writing about.

It is believed by this author that strategies taught by teachers can reduce aggressive behavior in resolving conflicts in schools. To this extent, aggressive behavior may assume many venues, each of which may be dealt with on their own terms. Conflict resolution has proven to be key in terms of providing resolutions for aggressive behavior, as has peer mediation, and shall be discussed at greater length in chapter II, that is Review of the Literature.

Throughout this dissertation, this author emphasizes a number of strategies that have proven useful within American schools throughout the United States, particularly at high school and elementary school levels. To this extent, such key terms as *aggressive, violent, adolescents, alternative programs, strategies, conflict resolution, mentoring,* and *peer mediation* shall be seen throughout this dissertation.

Many students are at high risk for school failure or display significantly challenging behaviors so that school officials have sought to have them educated in classrooms or facilities away from other students. This indeed has been one pervasive approach to coping with students who display aggressive behavior. Similarly and to this extent, this author proceeds to explore alternative education programs, serving students who display antisocial behavior, as well as discussion of the impact/research regarding alternative school placement on the setting of antisocial, violent, and aggressive behaviors within these settings.

The author provides some historical background, and during the 1980s and 1990s, there was a "zero tolerance" policy wherein many of America's schools assumed a "hard hand" in dealing with violent juveniles or adolescents. For example, knives, guns, and metal detectors were often the norm throughout many schools. However, as time went on, such approaches became more relaxed. At this point, this author should like to focus on why this author has chosen this topic or problem to research on. It is the intent to prove, on the part of this author, that effective strategies taught by teachers may reduce aggressive behavior in resolving conflicts in school.

This author speaks both from professional experience, observation, as well as (some) methods that have been tried. This author shall further expound, in the Methods (and to a lesser extent, the Findings), varied methods as relates to measuring and proving the efficacy of strategies that have been designed and formulated for exactly this purpose, that is, reducing aggressive behavior through the resolution of conflicts in schools. Ultimately, it is the intent of this author to prove the hypothesis that through effective strategies taught by teachers, we may evidence a dramatic reduction of aggressive behavior in resolving conflicts in the schools. To this extent, there exist a host of approaches that may be utilized.

Throughout this introduction or problem statement, this author should like to delve briefly upon some of those aforementioned strategies that this author believes to be of particular effectiveness. Schools and their curricula are subject to multiple requirements and demands. Because schools might not recognize the need for instruction in the reduction of violence and aggression, introducing effective programs into school curricula and schedules might be difficult. The need for teacher training for these programs also might make acceptance and implementation difficult; however, the benefits of many programs for traditional academic outcome, such as attendance and school performance, might enhance the interests of school policy makers, administrators, and teachers in these programs.

In summary, according to the authors, study results consistently indicated that universal school-based programs were associated with decreased violence. Beneficial results were found across all school levels examined, according to one study. On the basis of available economic data, universal school-based programs also appeared to be cost-effective.

Aggression develops in childhood and continues into adulthood. In this regard, Chamberlain even states that aggression can develop from before birth. Aggression starts within the psychological world of the individual. The way the individual interprets his/her perception will illicit an emotional response that will affect the person's decision on what to do with his/her interpretation of the world. What matters is the way it is expressed, either constructive or destructive behavior. Aggression is expressed in a constructive manner if it is about the survival, and personal and healthy growth of the individual, family group, and/or the community. Aggression is expressed in a destructive manner if it harms self, others, and/or the environment (Tesser, 1995).

The lack of student discipline in our public schools is a longstanding public concern of parents, school officials, and teachers alike. While disciplinary problems in our public schools may be a reflection of larger societal problems, there are clear indications that school discipline problems extend far beyond the classroom, affecting individual students, teachers, and the society at large and possibly having serious developmental implications. For example, research indicates that maladaptive aggressive responses to classroom social demands, occurring as early as the first grade, predict a host of maladaptive behavior, including antisocial behavior, criminality, and intravenous drug use later in life. Along these lines, research suggests that the lack of effective disciplinary procedures in the elementary school classroom—procedures that curtail aggressive behavior—may have important developmental consequences for future maladaptive behaviors (Kelam et al., 1983).

At this point, this author should like to interject what this author believes to be a central aspect of not only this dissertation but the schools in general. Schools should be regarded as both bastions for education, as well as the preparing of the students to be productive citizens. Especially when one views schools in this manner, it seems to this author that teachers, parents, school administrators, counselors, the community, civic leaders, and others would become more involved in curtailing aggressive behavior in the classroom.

Chapter II:
Review of Literature

As this author has indicated previously in the proposal for this dissertation, there will be great emphasis upon the effectiveness and the evaluation of effectiveness of conflict resolution programs in the classroom—the kinds of things in which teachers (especially new teachers) have to confront with what can be somewhat intimidating offenders in the classroom. Ultimately, based largely upon this literature review, this author shall be emphasizing the same for the purpose of ultimately evaluating strategies that have proven useful within America's schools, particularly in the high school and elementary school levels, for the purpose of establishing the findings (i.e., chapter IV) in a qualitative format as this author has previously indicated. Thus, key terms shall focus upon *aggressive, violent, behavior, children, adolescents, alternative programs, strategies,* and *conflict resolution,* largely based on the schools as so many have been.

It is the firm belief of this author that through the "sharing" of successful methods for curtailing aggressive behaviors in the schools, the many thousands of schools nationwide experiencing such problems—and they are many indeed—can help each other with both effective and innovative strategies and programs as those that schools have developed.

According to Van Acker (2007), who reports that the display of antisocial behavior by children and youth in America is recognized as one of the most pressing concerns facing educators today. To meet the educational needs of these students while maintaining safe school environments, school districts across the nation have increasingly looked toward alternative educational programs. Approximately 2% or roughly 280,000 youths attend alternative school in the United States (Grunbaum et al., 1999). For the most part, these students are at high risk for school failure or display significantly challenging behaviors so that school officials have sought to have them educated in classrooms or facilities away from other students. As a result, students with significant behavioral concerns of educational disabilities are clustered together into alternative educational programs. The author explores alternative education programs serving students who display antisocial behavior and discusses research on the impact of alternative school placement on the setting of antisocial, violent, and aggressive behaviors within these setting.

The author also focuses on the social context of the alternative school that might exacerbate the development of antisocial behavior and highlights empirically validated prevention and intervention efforts.

The United States has the highest youth homicide and suicide rates among the wealthiest developed nations. Homicide is the second leading cause of death for youths aged fifteen to nineteen-years, and suicide is the third. Sixteen million adolescents in the United States have witnessed some kind of violent assault in their lifetimes, including up to the 95% of inner-city children. Between 1980 and 2000, a dramatic rise in school violence and aggression resulted in public concern and several legislative responses to the problem (e.g., A Safe and Drug-Free Schools and Communities Act, the Guns-Free Schools Act of 1994).

Schools took action to curb the growth of antisocial, violent, and aggressive behaviors. Many schools adopted increased security methods, such as security guards, metal detectors, and video surveillance of public areas. Schools adopted zero-tolerance policies and often punished the target behavior (e.g., violence, aggression, truancy, substance abuse) with harsh and punitive consequences (e.g., suspension, expulsion). The rate of suspensions and expulsion skyrocketed across the United States (SKIBA, 2001). However, instead of reducing the rates of violence and aggression throughout the schools, these practices have escalated the problem. The tendency to criminalize school behavior is associated with increased school dropout ratios, higher levels of incarceration, and minority overrepresentation in juvenile detention (Van Acker, 2007, p. 9).

As the author indicated, alternative education programs are capable of meeting the needs of youth who display antisocial behavior by providing comprehensive services focused on individual needs and an effective treatment environment, removing students from ineffective and coercive school, home, and community influences and providing a safe setting for addressing their problem behaviors while promoting academic success; and establishing a routine discipline that can bring order to youths whose lives may have been chaotic.

For the most part, the best practices for alternative education rely on expert opinion and extrapolation of what has been effective in other educational settings. To this extent, it is the intent of this author to focus on what has been effective in other education settings, as this author is acutely aware that many programs (e.g., conflict resolution within the schools themselves) have proved to be highly successful in many cases. It seems to me that an important question/issue should address the causes of aggressive behavior.

According to one report, video games have an impact upon aggressive thoughts and behaviors. This was further validated during the now very infamous Columbine incident, that is, one of many wherein a group of young adolescent boys, as has been reported, spent much time interacting with exceedingly violent video games and animation prior to their reporting to schools with guns and opening up at random killing many people. However, the study in question examines the effects of playing a violent video game on aggressive thoughts and behavior and the moderating role of affective orientation in the violent video game—aggressive behavior relationship.

Approximately two weeks after having their effective orientation measures, fifty-nine participants (plus five additional participants) played a violent or nonviolent video game for ten minutes. Participants then performed a work-completion task and judged the researchers' competence, courtesy, and deservedness of financial support. The results show that participants who played the violent video game rated the researcher as less courteous and less deserving of financial support when compared with participants who played the nonviolent video game and that affective orientation and video game condition interacted to predict valuation of courtesy and deservedness of financial support.

Although numerous studies have shown that playing violent video games can elicit aggressive behavior (Anderson, 2003; Anderson et al., 2004), very few studies have taken into account the extent to which game players' personality traits may moderate these effects. Media scholars, however, recommend examining the role personality traits play in the media effects process. For example, Oliver (2002) suggested that "individual differences can play an important role in moderating the direction and nature of media influence . . . . The existence of certain individual characteristics may heighten or intensify media influences or may even provide the necessary conditions for media influences to occur."

Regarding media violence, Sparks and Sparks (2002) suggested that the role played by individual differences in the media violence—suggestive behavior link and the effects of violent video games on aggressive behavior will be the foci of future research. In regards to the effects of violent video games in particular, Anderson (2003) pointed out that although there are valid theoretical reasons to believe that different types of people may be more or less susceptible to video games' effects, researchers have not really addressed this issue. Given this paucity of issues, Anderson (2003) issued a call for research on this issue. (Chory-Assad and Cicchirillo, 2005, p. 12)

Prior to exploring strategies for curtailing aggressive behavior in schools, the author has been and would like to present some background as to some experimental studies, both quantitative and qualitative, as have been carried out and indicated heretofore, in order to establish a basic understanding of the hows and whys aggressive behavior is carried out in the classroom. This author has reviewed an enormous amount of literature and preselected those that this author believes are most relevant. For example, television has proved to show up as contributory to aggressive behavior. Even verbally aggressive behavior sitcoms might call to mind certain aggressive thoughts related to aggressive ideas in one's mind, according to Chory-Assad and Cicchirillo (2005). However, violent video game effects and content have been identified consistently as a crime causal effect on aggressive behavior in the classroom, as well as outside of the classroom.

More on Background/Reasons for Aggressive Behavior in the Classroom

According to a (published) report by Chattopabhyay et al., there exists a need, as the author believes would prove effective, for universal school-based programs to reduce or prevent violent behavior. These are delivered to all children in classrooms in a grade or in a school. Similarly, programs targeted to schools in high-risk areas (defined by low socioeconomic status or high crime rates) are delivered to all children in a grade or school in those high-risk areas.

During 2004-2006, the Task Force on Community Preventive Services conducted a systematic review of published scientific evidence concerning the effectiveness of this program. The results of this review provide strong evidence that universal school-based programs decrease rates of violence and aggressive behavior among school-aged children. The program effects were demonstrated at all grade levels. An independent meta-analysis of school-based programs confirmed and supplemented these findings. On the basis of strong evidence of effectiveness, the task force recommends the use of universal school-based programs to prevent violent behavior.

The prevention of youth violence and aggression is of value in itself and also because early violence and aggressive behavior is a precursor of later problem behavior. Researchers categorize risk factors for early childhood delinquency, including violent behavior, as individual, family, peer, neighborhood, and media. Factors in all categories are thought to contribute to the development of early and chronic violent behavior, and they are all thought to provide opportunity to intervention to reduce the development of these behaviors.

The more serious forms of violent crime (i.e., rape, sexual assault, robbery, aggravated assault, and homicide) rarely occur in schools. During July 1992 to 2000, an annual average of twenty-nine homicides and five suicides occurred throughout US schools, representing 1% of the homicides among youths aged five to nineteen years and 0.5% of suicides among youths away from schools during the same period. However, a disappointing amount of nonfatal crimes occurred in school localities or on the way to or from school. Although the rate of crime declined from 1993 to 2003, in 2003, approximately 740,000 violent crimes were committed at schools against adolescents twelve to eighteen years of age. Of these crimes, approximately 150,000 were classified as "serious" (Chattopadhyay, 2007, p. 11).

Schools and their curricula are subject to multiple requirements and demands. Because schools might not recognize the need for instruction in the reduction of violence and aggression, introducing effective programs into school curricula and schedules might be difficult. The need for teacher training for these programs also might make acceptance and implementation difficult; however, the benefits of many programs for traditional academic outcome, such as attendance and school performance, might enhance the interests of school policy makers, administrators, and teachers in these programs.

In summary, according to the authors, study results consistently indicated that universal school-based programs were associated with decreased violence. Beneficial results were found across all school levels examined. On the basis of available economic data, universal school-based programs also appear to be cost-effective.

Attitudes as Relates to Aggressive Behavior in Schools

As this author has already alluded to aggressive behavior and attitudes, as well as their causal effects, it is further the belief of this author that one report from education provides a more psychological sense of insight regarding aggressive behavior, stating that aggression is an internal process of the human being in relationship with his/her self, other persons, and the environment. The external manifestations of aggression, whether constructive or destructive, are not the starting point of aggression. Aggression develops from childhood and continues into adulthood.

In this regard, Chamberlain even states that aggression can develop from before birth. Aggression starts within the psychological world of the individual. The way the individual interprets his/her perception will illicit an emotional response that will affect the person's decision on what to do with his/her interpretation of the world. What matters is the way it is expressed, either through constructive of destructive behavior. Aggression is expressed in a constructive manner if it is about the survival and personal and healthy growth of the individual, family group, and/or the community. Aggression is expressed in a destructive manner if it harms self, others, and/or the environment (Tesser, 1995). According to Kruger et al. (1993), aggression can be viewed as any type of behavior that is directed to harm, hurt, inflict pain, or destroy another person when this person is motivated to avoid such behavior. Aggression can also be self-directed, consciously or unconsciously (self-critical, self-harm, verbal threats, and assault).

Psychosocial factors that contribute toward aggressive behavior include the inability to cope with frustration; exposure to aggressive models, such as violence in the media and parents with aggressive behavior; poor socioeconomic circumstances, especially in urbanized areas; poor family relationships; and times of social stress, such as high inflation rates, increasing divorce statistics, and rejection by peers (Pepler and Sedighdeilami, 1998).

Situational factors can contribute toward aggressive behavior, including competitive sports, physical pain, anxiety, being in a crowd, and air and noise pollutions. The author cites the self-determination theory, which states that the motivational orientation has been linked to how the individual regulates self-esteem in other potentially threatening contexts and social interactions (Hodgens et al., 1996). Furthermore, Deci and Ryan (1991) stated that when self-regulation proceeds according to an unintegrated aspect of the person, as with the ego involvement on controlled behavior, the experienced emotion will be less flexible, more pressured, and more subjective to defensive reaction that less fully expresses one's integrated self. (Myburgh, 2005, p. 8)

The author basically concluded that one of the challenges has to do with shaping children's physical reactivity to emotional states. An important component of emotional socialization is learning to regulate the physiological arousal that accompanies distressed emotional states. Empathy, the ability to mirror another person's emotions, is a prerequisite for most prosaic or altruistic behavior (Isenberg et al., 1992). Personal distress inhibits prosaically responding reactions and may disinhibit aggressive reactions.

Another author expounds on the necessity to prevent aggressive disruptive behavior in middle school, which the authors indicate must begin in elementary school. In the article The Clearinghouse published nearly fifteen years ago, the author Thomas R. McDaniel's (1996) discussion on school discipline opens as follows: "The Sixteen Annual Gallup poll of the public's attitude towards public schools indicated once again, for the fifteenth time, that discipline is believed to be the number one problem of American education."

Our public school environment is still plagued with disciplinary problems including talking, leaving desk without permission, passing notes, poking other students, making sarcastic and hostile remarks, or more seriously, cursing, using drugs, fighting, assaulting teacher, and carrying weapons to school (Elan and Rose, 1995). The lack of student discipline in our public schools is a long-standing public concern of parents, school officials, and teachers alike.

While disciplinary problems in our public schools may be a reflection of larger societal problems, there are clear indications that school discipline problems extend far beyond the classroom, affecting individual students, teachers, and the society at large and possibly having serious developmental implications. For example, research indicates that maladaptive aggressive responses to classroom social demands, occurring as early as first grade, predict a host of maladaptive behaviors, including antisocial behavior, criminality, and intravenous drug use later in life. Along these lines, research suggests that the lack of effective disciplinary procedures in the elementary school classroom—procedures that curtail aggressive behavior—may have important developmental consequences for future maladaptive behaviors (Kelam et al., 1983).

It is critical for educators to understand the major research on the developmental course of aggressive behaviors occurring in the early classroom environment. In addition, valuable prevention tools for teachers in mitigating later, more serious maladaptive behaviors are essential for educators (Greer-Chase et al., 2002, p. 8). According to the authors, there exists a strong suggestion throughout their report that the course and malleability of maladaptive behaviors are partly rooted in early aggressive behaviors occurring in poorly managed classrooms. (This author shall subsequently focus more on classroom strategies designed to curtail aggressive behavior.)

Given the severity of disciplinary problems in our public schools and the apparent lack of systematic classroom management training for future teachers, it behooves teacher education training programs to incorporate classroom management as a mandatory element of teacher preparation. The prevention of disciplinary problems and maladaptive behavior in public schools may rest in our effectively teaching prospective teachers how to manage their classrooms. Public school systems should also ensure that current teachers receive ongoing classroom management skills training, particularly in the early school years, when students are first learning to negotiate classroom demands. The nature and the severity of aggressive behavior and a host of serious maladaptive behaviors in middle schools may depend on effective classroom management by elementary school teachers.

To begin with, as this author has presented heretofore some theoretical analysis regarding aggressive behavior at its earliest stages, according to Gannon et al. (1998), the authors address decreasing violent and aggressive theme play among preschool children. In recent years, parents, teachers, and mental health professionals have expressed increased concern regarding the effect of aggressive stimuli and violent situations on young children's lives. This concern is based on mounting evidence that rates of verbal and physical aggression by children may be increased by viewing aggressive or violent acts (either live or enacted) or by having access to toys or games that represent violent or aggressive themes.

Early work on the effect of aggressive themes in children's play (Feshback, 1956) demonstrated that children who listened to an aggressive story and then where permitted to play with neutral toys engaged in more inappropriate or antisocial acts than the children who had listened to neutral stories. In 1971, Turner and Goldsmith found that the presence of toy guns, as opposed to the more novel ingressive toys, increased the rate of observed antisocial behavior in preschool free-play settings. Similarly, Etaugh and Happaugh (1979) found some degree of association between aggression-related play (hitting punching bags) and subsequent aggressive behavior directed toward peers.

Early childhood special educators frequently have recommend verbal prompts as a method for instructing children, as well as a strategy for reducing play involving inappropriate themes and content (Brophy et al., 1975). Verbal prompts typically includes an interruption of unacceptable or inappropriate behavior, followed by a suggestion that a child engage in an alternative, appropriate behavior, such as "Use the tinker toys to build cameras instead of guns" or "Can you think of another way to play?"

Several potential risks can be identified in the use of verbal prompts to reduce violent or aggressive theme play. First, provision of verbal prompts as a consequence may actually reinforce violent or aggressive theme play and serve to maintain these undesired behaviors. Second, the reinforcing qualities of these aggressive behaviors may be stronger than prompted alternative responses and thus might continue despite a teacher's skill at suggesting alternative responses (Gannon et al., 1998, p. 7). The authors conclude by stating that further investigations are needed to validate the effectiveness of this procedure in other community settings. Additional settings could further identify the elements that maintain violent or aggressive theme play. With a growing concern regarding the effect of this play on later developments, further investigations of this sort would be beneficial.

In the view of this author and as the rationale provided for such studies, this dissertation is intended to provide the teacher with the "most thorough" (and earliest) understanding of reasons for aggressive behavior.

Case Studies/Strategies in the Classroom for Curtailing and Preventing Aggressive Behavior

At this point, this author is primarily interested in ages K-12, with emphasis upon the older adolescents, who could be quite formidable in terms of their physicality and intimidation. It is this (general) age level, including elementary, middle, and high schools especially, with which this author is particularly interested in. However, there exists many strategies, as previously alluded to, that this author believes, as hypothesized, can be quite useful in preventing violent and disruptive behaviors, which runs counter to education throughout our country's schools, with particular emphasis upon the aforementioned age group, or for purposes of this dissertation, this author will refer to them for the most part throughout this dissertation as the early adolescent years, which allows for some degree of latitude throughout high schools, middle schools, and even elementary schools.

Indeed, it is a very serious problem, not only for the overall objective of education but also for the impact it has on teachers, especially new or younger teachers who don't know how to cope with the situation, not to mention the most important factor that has to do with educating and socializing young people who are, in fact, young adults, who within ten years or less, shall be confronted with "adult problems and responsibilities" and must be prepared to handle them. To this extent, this author should like to state that these factors should be most important and relevant throughout this dissertation.

In the view of this author, the responsibilities of schools include educating and socializing young people for both preparation as well as actuation as productive citizens within society. This all begins in school. With which in mind, this author should like to let this be the basis for subsequent discussion and analysis, especially regarding aggressive behavior in the classroom as well as effective strategies that can prevent and curtail the same. This author believes that the prevention (or *curtailing*, a less emphatic term) involves many, including teachers, social workers, school counselors, administrators, parents, and even the co-opting of other schools, as well as the community. To this extent, it is hoped by this author that singular, relevant, and important issues may be identified for the benefit of subsequent segments throughout this dissertation, especially the Methodology section, wherein this author shall provide suggestions and recommendations for preventing aggressive behavior in the schools.

Childhood and youth violence in the schools is a major concern in the United States. It is becoming an increasingly important social policy issue and a major public health concern, as evidenced by increased funding of research to identify the causes of child and youth violence and the provision of grants to support the development, the implementation, and the evaluation of prevention/intervention programs. For example, the entire March 2003 issue of *Developmental Psychology*, a major journal in the field of psychology, has been devoted to "violent children," focusing on developmental patterns, intervention, and public policy. The author outlines the social and psychological risk factors related to violence in schools and describes strategies and programs that bring families and schools together to prevent future violence.

Similarly, the author identifies specific risk factors that double the probability that the youth will commit a violent act, including the following:

1. The family has a history of criminal violence.
2. The youth has a history of being abused.
3. The youth belongs to a gang.
4. The youth abuses drugs or alcohol.

As the author adds, the odds triple when the above factors are combined with the following:

1. The youth uses a weapon.
2. The youth has been arrested.
3. The youth has a neurological problem that impairs thinking and feeling.
4. The youth has difficulties in school and has a poor attendance record.

Studies show that poor school performance and absenteeism are strongly associated with peer rejection, especially in early childhood. Another risk factor related to school violence is being a victim of school bullying or feeling rejected or disrespected (Stevens et al., 2001). To this extent, it is the belief of this author that "bullying" is a grossly underrated and non-attended reality that can virtually disrupt an individual's entire life, both in school and out of school. Furthermore, it can be the prime or sole cause of bad grades, psychological problems, and failure (in reference to all of the aforementioned factors as indicated as associated with aggressive behaviors in the school; Boulter, 2004, p. 11).

Finally and as pointed out by Boulter (2004), violence prevention is dependent upon family-school connections and family involvement in the school. Effective school-based strategies and programs that prevent future violence emphasize the importance of building a strong parent, school, and community partnership. Schools and parents together can successfully replace violence and aggressive behavior by teaching, modeling, and reinforcing pro-social behavior, such as altruism and empathy, plus effective coping and problem-solving strategies to deal with frustration and anger, as may emanate from overall aggressive behavior, violence, and bullying.

Schools that successfully reduce violence teach anger control and other violence prevention strategies to parents through workshops, encouraging parents to continue these practices in the home, and urging parents to give teachers feedback regarding successes as well as problems. Also, these informed parents insist on school attendance, find ways to facilitate their children's attachment to the school through active involvement, and make a commitment to education by participating in school activities and parent/community organizations.

Aggressive Behavior in Schools and Conflict Resolution as an Essential Strategy

Indeed, aggressive behavior can take many forms, and the teacher (as well as others, as previously indicated) must be prepared for the many variations of "aggressive behavior" as may occur. Indeed, it is important to understand the many types (variations) of aggressive behavior that may evidence itself especially and specifically in the classroom setting.

At the outset of this section (Review of Literature), this author made reference to conflict resolution and the fact that many schools have adopted their own "brand" of conflict resolution and implemented the same within the classroom setting. Indeed, many schools have experienced positive and successful results with conflict resolution in school, as this author should like to address. To this extent, this author should like to identify some schoolwide conflict resolution as well as peer mediation programs. For example and as reported by Dounic et al., effective schoolwide responses to disruptive, aggressive, and violent student behaviors are critical to ensuring teacher and student safety and to increasing constructive approaches to conflict. As such, many educators are implementing school-based prevention programs focused on conflict resolution (CR) and peer mediation (PM).

As disruptive, aggressive, and violent behaviors appear to be more prevalent throughout the school population, schoolwide approaches to discipline are critical to ensuring safety and increasing appropriate student school interaction. Classroom teachers often have available options when faced with disruptive or aggressive actions. In addition, administrative decisions in dealing with inappropriate behavior are frequently punitive, resulting in student suspension from school or in placement in alternative school settings, yet few professionals would agree that punitive reactions to disruptive, violent, or aggressive acts teach appropriate behavior or are effective in the long term.

In response to the need for appropriate and more proactive discipline plans, many educators are implementing school-based prevention programs focused on CR and PM. CR programs typically include a curriculum designed to teach students to acknowledge individual differences, change win-lose paradigms to win-win solutions, and use negotiations to resolve conflicts (Carlsson-Paige and Levin, 1992). Interventions based on conflict resolution may also include specific information on mediation of conflict by typically trained peers. Peer mediation is a structure process consisting of specific steps to help disputants define and solve a problem and move away from dependence on punitive, seclusionary methods. It includes an attempt to affect how students conceptualize conflict. Proponents suggest that an effective PM program can do the following:

1. Provide students with a framework for solving conflicts.
2. Give students an opportunity to assume responsibility for their own behavior.
3. Lower teacher stress by reducing the number of student conflicts they have to handle.
4. Increase instruction on hand.
5. Help students understand how cultural diversity can affect interpersonal communication and human interaction.

Over the past three years, the authors have investigated the effectiveness of a schoolwide CR curriculum and PM program. Working in three middle schools in the US South East, the authors specifically examined the protocols necessary for implementing a successful media program—factors that facilitated its effectiveness and the way students learned to manage their peer conflicts. From a theoretical base, according to Johnson and Johnson (1996), the conceptual underpinnings of CR/PM programs are rooted in developmental and sociopsychological theories.

Students at the middle school level value peer relationships highly and are heavily influenced by them. Moreover, students entering adolescence have increasing independence and identity needs. Those who develop positive and adequate mechanisms for coping with the complex demands of their environment have an excellent chance of growing into emotionally healthy adults. Successful coping requires acquisition of new approaches to challenging situations when outmoded responses stop working. Developmental psychologists call this process of creating new cognitive structure "accommodation" (Berger, 1984), which takes place most readily when we provide optimal levels of both challenge and support.

A significant change for middle school students is learning to resolve conflicts with their peers. Teaching students problem-solving skills through a schoolwide conflict resolution program that includes PM can help resolve the inevitable conflicts they encounter in the school environment, increase their self-esteem, and foster independence. CR/PM allows students to have a "say" in how their disputes are resolved. Moreover, as they learn about effective communication, anger management, and taking another's perspective—subjects taught in a typical CR curriculum—students generally become less likely to engage in aggressive or destructive behavior. We also have reason to believe that an effective PM program can improve school climate.

The program initiated by the author occurred at three middle schools in the South East and is a schoolwide approach consisting of two components:

1. a school-wide CR curriculum
2. a PM program that enlists a core group of trained peer mediators in each school

Using the schoolwide curriculum, teachers can inform students of the rationale for informed conflict resolution and introduce them to appropriate negotiation procedures. Teachers can also help students understand viable alternatives to more constructive ways to handling day-to-day conflicts. The essential tenet of our curriculum is that conflict is an inevitable part of any social environment and that students can address conflict through a problem-solving framework.

All three schools identified a cadre of twenty to thirty-five students across the three grade levels to mediate disputes throughout the year. The project also consisted of personnel-trained groups of four to six teachers and/or guidance counselors throughout the schools that were responsible for training the selected students. The peer mediators were trained over a two-day period in skills related to understanding conflict, confidentiality, effective communication, listening, and the mediation process. Beginning with a discussion of topics overlapping those included in the schoolwide curriculum, the training focused on the structured mediation process, including associated role plays. Students who successfully completed the training were designated officially as schoolwide peer mediators for the year.

The school would use conflict referral forms to record relevant information, such as the referring party, the conflict location, a brief problem description, and the disputants' names. An agreement form signed by both mediators and the students was used at the conclusion of each mediation. The mediation form included the mediation date, the type of conflict, and the agreed upon resolution. Although a teacher or counselor was expected to be available during the mediation process, in the event that adult intervention became necessary, we encourage school personnel to minimize routine supervision to ensure confidentiality.

School-based administrators and CR/PM teams should consider infusing conflicts resolution into the school curriculum on an ongoing basis. In our project, we originally intended to provide a yearlong comprehensive curriculum designed to continue and inform students of constructive approaches to dispute resolution through a substantial amount of practice in recognizing and dealing effectively with anger. Because of continuous demands on teacher's time and the constraints of already-crowded class schedules, school administrators requested that we condense the material into five lessons. We believe that such a brief exposure to content designed to alter attitudes and behavior seriously limits program effectiveness

In conclusion, according to Daunic et al. (2000, p.11), in a school that has a committed administrator, an implementation team invested in the program's success, and a schedule that facilitates the mediation process and its supervision, CR/PM programs can alter student responses to conflict in a positive way. Indeed, in what we judged to be the most effectively implemented program, we saw a decline in overall office referral and in referral specifically for disruptive and aggressive behaviors.

Although the research base for CR/PM is still in its infancy, we are cautiously optimistic that well-designed CR/PM programs can have far-reaching effects on students' attitudes and behaviors. Some evidence shows that PM can benefit interpersonal relations among students, teachers, and administrators and thus have a substantial impact on school discipline. Moreover, when students generalize what they have learned, they may incorporate negotiation, mediation, and problem solving in family and community settings as well.

Overall, it is the belief of this author that both conflict resolution programs as well as peer mediation programs are among the most effective in terms of practical strategies for the classroom teacher when coping with student aggressive behavior. Indeed, this author should like to further explore both conflicts resolution and peer mediation separately and inclusively, as this author already had introduced same (i.e., inclusively), while many school throughout the nation have implemented one or both programs, that is, CR and/or PM, either separately or together.

It is also indeed the view of this author that involving older students to work with younger ones (i.e., peer mediation) would be of particular value. That is to say that junior and senior members of a respective high school would likely be the best candidates for implementing peer mediation for the benefit of reconciling or preventing aggressive behavior.

As previously indicated in the aforementioned case studies, there does indeed exist training and organized programs for peer mediation (as well as conflicts resolution) wherein upon completion, an individual is that much more prepared to help the teacher, the school, and the educational system conduct an effective academic program—much as the school is designed for. At this point, this author also believes it is worth reiterating that the school must be regarded as a bastion for educating students as well as preparing them for post-education period and infusion into society as productive citizens.

Overall and to a large extent, this author shall be addressing both conflict resolution as well as peer mediation selectively or together. As previously indicated, conflict resolution and peer mediation projects have been and continue to be conducted throughout schools nationwide for many years now, wherein they have had ample time to refine the process and, indeed, have reported highly successful results. Many US schools are implementing curricula and other activities to reduce interpersonal violence among students, which involved conflict resolution or peer mediation training.

Frankly, as this author has identified through the very extensive literature review, some reports indicate that little is known about the effectiveness or manner of implementing CR/PM training, while others seem to be quite seasoned in this area and have long since gone on to highly successful implementation projects, as is the case throughout hundreds, if not thousands, of schools throughout the United States as of this writing.

Nevertheless, according to the authors as cited, available data suggest that some projects may modify youth's self-reported attitudes about violent behavior, improve school discipline, and reduce absenteeism. The review also reveals considerable consideration in implementation, especially in the role of professionally trained consultants and the amount of teacher and student training. More attention should be paid to evaluating CR/PM projects. Some data suggest that they may contribute positively to community efforts to reduce violence among youths, but insufficient information exists to know what projects best serve which students and how a project should be implemented.

Interpersonal violence among youth represents a major problem across the United States. Homicide victimization and perpetration rates for young males aged fifteen to nineteen are increasing substantially since 1985. Similarly, physical fighting, weapon carrying, assault, robbery, and sexual assaults are too common among youths. As violence becomes a more prevalent concern for society, safety at school becomes an issue as well. To create a safer atmosphere at school and to contribute to broader efforts within the community to reduce violence, a large but unknown number of US schools have implemented a project to reduce interpersonal violence among youths. Estimates place a number of schools adopting some sort of violence prevention training at more than 5,000. These efforts provide cognitive, behavioral, and social skills training on various topics using sundry methods.

Although other terms sometimes are used for the projects, they commonly are referred to as conflict resolution and peer mediation (CR/PM) training. While conflict resolution and peer mediation often are talked about and implemented together, they differ. Conflict resolution training, as commonly implemented and as used in this paper, provides training to an entire class, grade, or school. In contrast, peer mediation training is provided to a few selected students. In general, conflict resolution programs teach youths to manage anger, control aggressive responses, understand conflict, and avoid and diffuse potentially physically violent confrontations. Peer mediation projects train a few selected students to mediate disputes between other students. Student mediators are taught to remain impartial. They generally are the same age as the disputants. Both conflict resolution and peer mediation allow students to settle disagreements peacefully among themselves.

One useful case study, in the view of this author, took place in Florida, where a CR/PM skills training project was piloted at one elementary school (K-6) in the greater metropolitan Miami area. The project was supported by the Florida Department of Health and Rehabilitative Services, the Florida Injury Prevention and Control Program, the Dade County Public Health Unit, the Dade/Monroe Teacher Education Center, and the Peace Education Foundation. The school enrolls approximately 1,700 students, 90% of whom are members of minority groups and 85% of whom qualify for a free or reduced-price lunch. The violent crime rate in 1992 in Dade County was 19.1 per 1,000 population.

The curriculum, Fighting for Model, was designed by the Peace Education Foundation and is based on age and grade-appropriate workbooks and materials previously developed by the same organization. It teaches students to deal with conflict positively and to replace aggressive behaviors with constructive ones. The curriculum contains The Rules for Fighting Fair, which students are to adopt in conflict-provoking situations. The rules are

1. identify the problem;
2. focus on the problem;
3. attack the problem not the person;
4. listen with an open mind;
5. treat a person's feeling with respect;
6. take responsibility for your actions.

Negative or destructive behaviors such as name calling, threats, or hitting are termed "fouls." Students learn through their hands-on techniques including role playing, brainstorming, puppetry, classroom discussion, stories, and skits. Students also learn to mediate between others. The importance of listening, questioning, and paraphrasing skills are explained and then reinforced through interactive exercises and mock mediation.

An educational specialist with the Dade Monroe Teacher Education Center served as the project coordinator. She conducted a three-day workshop to familiarize teachers in the experimental group with the concepts of conflict resolution and to teach them how to use the curriculum. She visited classrooms and met with the teachers at least weekly to conduct demonstration lessons and to ensure that the curriculum was being implemented consistently. During the seven-week implementation period, teachers in the experimental group introduced conflict resolution into the language, arts, and social studies curriculum through almost daily thirty-minute lectures. Students were directed to solve interpersonal disputes using knowledge obtained through these sessions.

Other methods of introducing conflict resolution into the community and reinforcing it among students include

1. project updates for the PTA and local community planning committees;
2. field trips for the student mediators to the FBI headquarters, the Circuit Court of Baltimore, and Coppin State College;
3. a school poster contest involving a conflict mediation theme;
4. a conflict resolution training workshop for local children at a community summer recreation center, conducted by the project coordinator using student mediators for their knowledge and skills.

During the training, students learn about the roles and the responsibilities of a mediator. They discuss events that frequently result in conflict and the consequences of various responses. Using role playing and mock mediation, mediators learn the skills needed to help disputants reach a resolution. Finally, students discuss methods for introducing conflict mediation to the entire school. The students are referred to mediation by teachers and other students. The mediation process takes place in the counselor's office. Student mediators have disputants tell their sides of the problem and then encourage the disputants to generate a solution. A mutually agreed upon solution is written, which the disputants sign. The school counselor is available in the mediation area but does not participate in the mediation. The mediation sessions occur throughout the day during class time and last fifteen to thirty minutes each.

Another case study this author should like to identify is taking place in North Carolina, wherein a conflict resolution project in a middle school (grades 6-8) in Orange County, North Carolina, was supported by the injury control section, Division of Epidemiology, North Carolina Department of Environmental Health and Natural Resources. The school has a population of more than 700 students, approximately 29% of whom are members of a racial or ethnic minority; 21% qualify for a free or reduced-cost lunch. The violent crime rate in Orange County is 14.8 per 1000 population.

The curriculum involved a combination of conflict resolution and peer mediation training, incorporating aspects of several existing projects. A trainer from the Orange County Dispute Settlement Center to teach 391 sixth-grade students about conflict resolution during three 15-minute classroom periods. Nine teachers also were trained in conflicts resolutions theory. With lectures, discussion groups, and role playing, students would talk about individuality, anger, and power. Then they were introduced to the concept that self-control is having "power" to remain calm when upset or angry. Teens were taught The Rules for Fighting Fair, also used in Florida (Halasyamani et al., 1995, p. 9).

Ultimately, what the authors concluded was the following recommendations based on information from nine projects conducted in four states including the following:

1. Evaluations of CR/PM projects are needed. These projects are being widely implemented at unknown costs and with unconfirmed benefits.
2. Given the limited evidence of success, the burgeoning number of curricula, and the wide range of implementation efforts, school officials should assess the success of any project adopted by the school. Assessment need not be expensive or exhaustive, but it should be done.
3. Evaluation should describe the target group; the comparison group; the content of the curriculum; the project implementation, including the role of the consultant; and many other factors such as involvement of parents or provision of mentors.

Conflict resolution and conflict resolution training has also been identified as an alternative to suspension for "aggressive behavior" (the authors also utilize the term *violent behavior*). The structuring format of the Alternative to Suspension for Violent Behavior (ASVB) is predicated on research findings that have provided substantial evidence that violence is largely learned and consequently can be prevented through teaching alternative to violence (Eden et al., 1994). This theory does not deny that the factors contributing to violence are varied and that no one factor is the sole cause of violence. For example, although it is true that some acts of violence do result from extreme anger or lack of impulse control, still "inadequate impulse control puts an individual at risk for violence only if violent acts are that person's preferred response choice because of previous learning experiences."

Several model programs also include parent training because research has shown that some of the most significant risk factors for violence originate in the family. It is critical to make the ASVB a family intervention. Reed (1981) found that the family affected students' attitudes and belief about conflict, and he identified lack of parental supervision, responsibility, and involvement as the most influential family issues. Weissberg and Greenberg (1987) linked poor parenting skills and family disharmony with adolescent problems. Engaging the family in changing its beliefs and practices about conflict and violence can contribute to changing a students' use of violence.

Because there is no program in existence at the secondary level that could be readily adapted for the ASVB, we created our own, incorporating the practices just described. The skill-building and thinking skills components are grounded in the conflict resolution theory. The ASVB uses a thirty-six-page skills manual titled *Making the Smart Choice: Truth for Resolving Conflict*. The manual is covered in six hours, generally spread over forty 90-reim sessions. Our assessment of how much effort families would invest in their turn for a reduced suspension dictated the six-hour time frame for the program.

The core premises and skills of conflict resolution are derived from the principles and the practices of mediation. Mediation begins with the premise that conflict is inevitable and destructive only when it is handled inappropriately. Furthermore, the mediator assumes that the parties in the conflict are deadlocked because the positions they adopt are irreconcilable; in other words, the only allowable outcome result is one person winning and the other person losing.

Violence enters into a conflict either when the winner uses violence to get his or her way or when the loser reacts to defeat with violence. The goal of conflict resolution strategy is to find the solution to the conflict whereby both parties get what they want and avoid violence in the process. Attempting to do this by reconciling opposing positions usually leads to further polarization; therefore, the parties must learn to articulate the needs that underlie their position. The negotiation can then take place around the respective needs of the parties. As long as the needs of both sides are met, they can drop their positions and therefore have a satisfying outcome.

These premises of conflict resolution are easy to articulate and accept, but implementing them requires considerable cognitive skill. The cognitive skills that are required are perspective taking and active listening. On most measures reported, students who participated in the ASVB fared better than those who did not. They were suspended less frequently for physical and nonphysical violence, their DAI scores were lower, and they were not expelled, whereas seven students from the pooled nontreatment group were expelled.

The goal of the ASVB—to reduce violence by providing a secondary prevention program for at risk, late-onset offenders—appears to have been modestly met. Similarly, the ASVB has several attractive features for schools. First, because it is an off-campus program, attendance does not result in any missed classes. Second, because of its fee-for-service arrangement, it costs the school very little. Local agencies wishing to strengthen their ties to a high school bear the cost to set up and deliver the program. These costs may well be offset by the lower administrative costs that result because students who complete the program are disciplined less frequently.

However, the study, like so many others, underscores the efficacy of conflict resolution training. Similarly and as previously cited and according to the previous studies cited, many have found conflict resolution training and implementation a viable and effective alternative to suspension for violent or aggressive behavior.

Previously, this author made reference to the cultural imperative or what one author referred to as the cross-cultural conflict resolution in the schools. In the view of this author, as the demography and profile of America have increasingly taken on much more varied images in terms of people's ethnicity and their cultural background, CR/PM is more important than ever in the view of this author and more effective as well when oriented or directed to cross-cultural conflict resolution (in the schools). At this point, this author should like to identify some conflict resolution strategies, particularly in light of what the authors state, which has everything to do regarding acts of violence and terror that have now become pervasive in our culture.

School violence continues to be an area where many experts agree that much must be done to protect children and help them cope with the effects. Many children are afraid to go into the restroom or out into the playground because of the level of violence in school settings. According to statistics published by the Center for Disease Control (CDC, 1993), 28% of shootings happened inside a school building, 36% of violent events happened outside school property, and 35% happened off campus, and since 1992, the total number of multiple-victim events have increased significantly (CDC, 1992).

Nevertheless, direct strategies for the benefit of preventing and curtailing aggressive behavior in the classroom are paramount with this author and throughout this dissertation. Thus, regarding conflict resolution strategies, there is increasing interest in creating and improving the conflict resolution approach in public schools in the United States. Conflict resolution refers to the process of communication between two or more groups that are resolving a dispute with the help of a mediator. The mediator seeks to terminate the conflict and restore social relations between the groups to some level of legitimacy.

Attempts are made to help some people refrain from assigning blame and instead to focus on understanding the origins of the dispute and to find common ground for consensus. Lederach (1995) suggested that conflicts are constituted largely by the taken-for-granted common sense understanding that people have about their world, including themselves and the other people that inhabit it. Such common sense includes knowledge about what is viewed as right and wrong, how to proceed, whom to turn to, and where and with what expectations. Mediators also help to have people develop a better understanding of each other's positions to develop a relationship based on mutual respect and to encourage parties to reflect on one another's viewpoints in such a way that they will be more willing to resolve their disputes.

There are a number of conflict resolution tasks to follow in resolving disputes among groups of students. The most common programs used in schools often involve peer mediation and process curriculum (Bodine, 1984). The peer mediation approach is a conflict resolution program that uses a limited number of teen students who mediate school disputes and, it is hoped, disseminate their experience to others. The process curriculum approach uses a specific class time to teach student conflict resolution concepts and skills.

In one model, for example, students are helped to define their definitions of the problem, exchange perspective, and then figure out how to solve the problem through the use of consensus seeking (Ofier and Fox, 2001). With the use of these approaches, a lack of emphasis on cross-culture conflict resolution is noticeable. This fact alone concerns teachers and counselors who frequently engage in conflict resolution strategies with children of culturally and linguistically diverse backgrounds. Many of these children could benefit from approaches that consider the cultural and linguistic aspects of their experience.

As the diversity of the student population increases, so do the cultural conflicts that are exacerbated by the difference in language, culture, value system, and socioeconomic status between minority students and their mainstream counterparts and between minority subcultures. The consequence of these values and behavioral differences often leads to strained interpersonal relationships among and between groups. Given that the conflict resolution is an important function of counselors working in school settings, it would be helpful to have a set of strategies for working with culturally diverse populations. This is especially important when introducing novel ways of looking at conflicts, helping students to respond more respectfully, clarifying the underlying issues involved, and finding resources that might be useful to the parties. A prerequisite to using such problem-solving methods is learning what techniques, strategies, and roles to use in conflict situations and when to use them.

The authors introduce several cross-culture conflict resolution techniques and strategies that have worked when working with culturally and linguistically diverse students. The authors evaluated representative techniques in the United States, Asia, the Middle East, Africa, Western Europe, and the Pacific Islands. Although many of these ideas may seem unusual to counselors operating form their dissimilar cultural and linguistic perspectives, it is contended that most of the techniques have significant therapeutic value for increasing the likelihood of problem resolution in cross-cultural problem solving.

Cross-cultural conflict resolution rests on several philosophical assumptions. Each assumption encompasses the notion that the counselor must place the professional emphasis on cross-cultural problem solving, with recognition of and respect for individual differences and commonalities. First, when trying to resolve conflicts among and between groups, it is important for the counselor to define, understand, and make sense of conflicts within the cultural context of the groups involved in the dispute. In this regard, it is important to have an understanding of their techniques to resolve a dispute.

Second, overreliance on traditional problem-solving techniques and strategies when working in cross-cultural situation could increase vulnerability to emotional and behavioral problems. Huang and Ying (1989) pointed out that those situations can occur when traditional conflict resolution strategies are used in cross-cultural problem situations. Also, cross-cultural strategies provide a framework for understanding the role that culture had in influencing human behavior and interaction and, consequently, how culture can affect the problem-solving process.

The authors further make reference to "selective cross-cultural techniques and strategies, identifying traditions of the African culture of the Semai. Disputes between individuals in the community are the concern and the responsibility of every member of the tribe (Robarchek, 1997). As such, anyone who is aware of a conflict between individuals and the tribe has a duty to bring it to the attention of the head man or, in the case of a school setting, the counselors. The head man originates the *becharaa*, which is a form of assembly to resolve the dispute. For the becharaa, the head man summons the disputants, their kindred (or supporters), and any interested spectators to engage in a full discussion and debate of the conflict.

Furthermore, they begin with several discussions among everyone present about recent events, activities, and anything else other than the dispute that has brought them together. Eventually, an elder or influential member of the community shall present a long monologue focusing on formal affirmations of the interdependence of the group and the necessity of group unity. Others present may follow with similar affirmations. All of this sets the stage for any specific discussion of the particular conflict. The discussion and debate continue until there is nothing left to say.

The authors take several lessons from the becharaa; that is, counselors have neither the authority nor the desire to intervene in the same decisive way that a head man could; nevertheless, there are some intriguing methods to be learned from this cultural practice. For one thing, they have strong emphasis on community responsibility for conflict—they do not belong to the individual. Second, during the resolution phase, the disputants do not address one another but rather speak to their peers. This sort of collective responsibility emphasizes the systemic nature of interpersonal conflict that it is not simply a dispute between two individuals, but it involves many others in myriad ways.

The authors proceed to identify conflict resolution as it exists among many other cultures throughout the world, concluding that racially and economically diverse students who helped design the new policy found it difficult to believe that a few "privileged" kids were now challenging the policy that received strong support from students and administrators. The students opposing the policy were labeled "spoiled brats," "rich nerds," and other derogatory names.

On several occasions, the conflict was prevented from erupting into a major fight involving fists and weapons. To resolve the conflict, the school counselor intervened and formed two groups of students. One group represented those who were in favor of the current policy, while the other group wanted the policy modified to accommodate first-time offenders. The tension was so high between the groups that the counselor appointed a well-respected student advisor to serve as a kind of mediator.

Ultimately, conflict resolution strategies that incorporate cultural nuances should be incorporated into the evolving leadership roles of counselors in schools and elsewhere. Counselors should be trained to provide such mentoring and leadership, establishing an atmosphere that is receptive to diverse cultures. Of course, this would mean that to prevent and deal with issues of aggression and violence, counselors would have to be a lot more creative and innovative in their approaches, which may not be as difficult as it sounds, considering how relatively ineffective traditional methods have been in dealing with these issues (Brinson, 1994, p. 11).

This author would concur wholeheartedly regarding the special necessity and provisions when it comes to CRPM vis-à-vis cross-cultural training. For example, this author has found from personal experience that it is very useful to begin by identifying the demographic makeup of the class. Then, perhaps, put up pictures and posters and encourage students to participate. Asian students can put up Asian pictures of their choice; African American students can put up pictures of anyone from Martin Luther King and Nelson Mandela to anyone they want; Vietnamese students can put up pictures of their individual cultural choice; and the same with Irish, Japanese, Filipino, etc. and the whole spectrum of the (possible) cultural gamut that may appear within any given classroom. The same should be encouraged for other classes throughout the school.

Peer Mentoring

At this point, as this author has made reference to both conflict resolution (CR) and peer mediation (PM), this author has discussed both in tandem, while in point of fact, they are technically not the same as per this author's previously stated definition(s). Consequently and at this juncture, this author should like to address peer mediation in greater detail. This shall also address peer mentoring, especially given its "proximity" to peer mediation as measured by academic performance, persistence in school, self-esteem, and those dynamics that appear relevant as well as pervasive throughout the literature, especially experimental studies.

Peer mentoring means different things to different people, while for the "central" purpose of this literature review, this author is particularly interested with students helping students while an important benefit has been found among co-teaching and educators mentoring students. The mentoring relationship between faculty/

staff mentors and college students' protégés was examined to identify differences in how each participant evaluated their relationship.

Question and data from 205 faculty/staff mentors and 182 student protégés were analyzed. Hypothesized differences in perceptions of mentors and protégés were generally supportive. While students were more positive than their mentors in assessing the overall value of mentoring relationship, they were relatively unaware that mentors might enter into the relationship to obtain benefits to the mentors. Assessments of mentoring were unrelated to gender or to either status of either the mentor or the protégé.

The research on mentoring in educational settings ranges broadly from peer mentoring in secondary education to studies of faculty-graduate mentoring in doctoral programs (Franke and Dahlgren, 1996). The mentoring itself takes on a variety of forms. In some cases, formal programs are administered in which students are assigned to mentors (Campbell and Campbell, 1997). In others, students and mentors develop relations "naturally," with no formal structure nor support from the administration (Campbell, 2000, p. 10).

Colleges and universities are constantly dealing with issues of access, quality, and diversity that have the potential to divide faculty, staff, and students. The university is dedicated to developing intellectual and cultural values through quality academic programs, out-of-class experiences, and active learning. We strive to provide all students with the in-class knowledge and out-of-class experiences to help students achieve their education goals. Students should have appreciation for other persons, cultures, and ideas, which may be different than our own. As more and more nontraditional students come to the university, changes have to be made to meet the needs of all students in a multiversity.

For the purposes of developing effective retention programs among colleges and universities, colleges and universities not only provide increased access to their campuses but also foster a learning environment where students are given the opportunity to succeed. Persistence in college is a process of social and intellectual integration that leads to the development of competent community members. Social integration relates to involvement with peers, faculty, and university activities, while academic integration relates to academic performance, involvement with curriculum, and contact with faculty and staff.

Effective retention programs focus on providing students with positive social and academic experiences to ensure the success of all students, not just the academically gifted. To this extent, it is believed that peer mentoring serves a direct and important role. Accordingly, the FYI program has been designed to increase student satisfaction, success, and ultimate graduation. The program accomplishes these objectives through several university-wide efforts:

1. peer mentoring;
2. mandatory student orientation course within each academic college;
3. new student assessment;
4. advising programs.

Program activities encourage high academic performance, responsible citizenship, and culture sensitivity (Manns 2001, p. 9). Overall, it is the belief that co-mentoring, especially as relates to academic performance, is increasingly understood in a number of variables that, to a large extent and in the view of this author, are best understood in terms of culture and context, size of institution, values, lack of student involvement, strategies for building and maintaining community, increasing access and diversity, expanding leadership opportunities, and developing effective retention programs.

At this point, this author should like to interject that peer mentoring reflects a nexus among academic achievements, persistence in school, as well as self-esteem. It is also the belief that this will come to be reflected throughout this literature review and as seen at the conclusion. In fact, one report indicates how one primary goal of education is to help students gain the knowledge and the skills necessary to solve the problems that will occur in life.

One of the most touted methods for doing this is curriculum integration (McBee, 2000). This is not a stretch from peer mentoring. The concept of integrated curricula has been around since the nineteenth century and is once again at the forefront of educational change. Those who are leading this movement claims that an integrated curriculum is far superior to one that is compartmentalized and discipline based. Among the leaders of the movement are educational psychologists who claim that an integrated curriculum, by design, reaches more students by being taught a wide variety of learning styles. There exists a national curriculum standard for math, science, and physical education that support interdisciplinary collaboration. The "connection standard" of the National Council of the Teachers of Mathematics (MCTM, 2000) emphasized the importance of students being able to "recognize and apply mathematics in contexts outside of mathematics."

Developing and implementing an integrated curriculum is beneficial to students. American students rank in the lower 25% percentile for science and math when compared to students from other industrialized nations (Roth, 1993). "Upon graduation, the same students are ill prepared to enter the workforce and to become productive members of a fast-paced, technologically advancing society" (Hurd, 1991). One explanation is that the current discipline-based curriculum covers most topics at a contextual level, while very few topics are covered in great depth. The result is that students obtain only superficial knowledge of the material that they are required to know to be successful on their next text.

An integrated curriculum in which students are required to make connections using higher-order thinking skills and to demonstrate an acquired knowledge and understanding through projects and performances has been proposed as an effective way to raise student performance. An integrated curriculum also teaches students how to work on a team. This skill becomes increasingly important as more businesses adopt the team approach. Teachers reported that the students' focus changed from competition to cooperation because of the team concept. This led to a greater sense of responsibility because the students knew that their work affected their teammates' grades as well as their own. Consequently, students increased their peer mentoring and showed more concern for their peers' academic performance and understanding (Smith, 2004, p. 14).

Integrating curricula has received positive results, as has peer mentoring. Giving individuals (students) a greater reason to succeed, especially among their peers, and a sense of increased accountability serves to advance the very concept that is peer mentoring.

Another report underscores the integration of curriculum and its direct academic performance upon students. Within the study at issue, the curricula largely involve sport and physical activity programs, which were seen to provide an effective vehicle for which personal and social developments in young people can positively be effective. The report at issue summarized the main findings and identified and described programs that used sporting activities to reduce antisocial behavior in youth across one country (Australia).

One hundred seventy-five organizations replied to a questionnaire seeking information about their programs. About one-third of these programs were created with the aim of decreasing antisocial behavior. There is a view that providing an activity where previously there was none is more important than the type of activity provided. While young people often join sporting activities for fun, fitness, and contest, over 80% of the program surveyed in this study focused on young people at risk of drug use or criminal behavior or youth already exhibiting behavior of the type. These participants were often referred to the programs by school or by the criminal justice system.

Two themes emerged in relation to program conception and connection: meeting youth needs and decreasing antisocial behavior. Increasingly, preventing boredom was not a common knowledge articulated by the programs either in the conception of the program or in its intended outcomes. Boredom may, however, be implicitly included in other categories, such as meeting youth needs and providing positive alternatives. To achieve these goals, programs use a variety of methods, including diversionary activities, providing access to services, providing leadership skills, and building self-esteem while involving local communities. At this point, this author should like to identify self-esteem as one of the tertiary themes in this thesis.

As most programs offer a combination of activities, it is difficult to determine whether particular types of sport, physical activity, or outdoor experience is more or less likely to be associated with discrete aspects of the program from its conception, delivery, or intended outcomes. However, the analysis does suggest that providing an activity will be more important than the type of activity provided. This is because the activity is a mechanism for diverting use for antisocial behavior. This is consistent with the findings of some researchers who have found that providing an activity where previously there has been none is more important than the type of activity provided (Catalano et al., 1998; Makkai, 2004, p. 9).

It was concluded that sport and physical activity programs, as well as other academic activities, can facilitate personal and social development through which behavior may be positively affected. It seems to be primarily achieved by focusing on improving underlying risk factors that predispose individuals to such behavior.

Throughout this literature review and as indicated at the outset, this author is primarily concerned with the impact of peer mentoring as measured by academic performance, persistence in school, and self-esteem. High levels of self-esteem and positive school, peer, and family connections represent protective factors against youths' involvement in risky behavior. According to the report in question, findings from one of the Healthy Kids Mentoring Program, a multidisciplinary mentoring program for fourth-grade students in a Midwestern public school, twenty fourth-grade students were admitted into the program based on findings from a fifty-five-item survey distributed to all fourth graders ($N = 283$) regarding overall self-esteem, school, peer and family connectiveness, and involvement in risky behavior. The program, which ran from January 2000 to May 2000, consisted of four components:

1. relationship building
2. self esteem enhancement
3. goal setting
4. academic assistance

Pretest-posttest data show significant improvements at posttest in mentored students' self-esteem levels and positive connections to school, peers, and families. Mentored students also were significantly less likely to be depressed or involved in bullying and fighting at posttest than at pretest. Compared to nonmentored students, mentored students reported significantly higher school and family connectiveness scores at posttest. Research indicates high self-esteem serves as a protective factor to youth involvement in a risky health behavior. High self-esteem is associated with high academic achievement, involvement in sport and physical activity, and development of effective coping and peer-pressure resistance skills.

Similar to self-esteem, a sense of a positive school, peer, and family connectiveness protects youth from engaging in negative self-behavior. Positive social conditions decrease risk-taking behavior by providing youth with pro-social and empowering opportunities. Youth who feel supported and cared for by parents, teachers, and peers report feeling most efficacious in making healthy, informed decision and displaying features of resiliency to potential life stressors. Students spend a large portion of their time in school, so school-based health education and prevention programs need to be implemented for the purpose of increasing youth self-esteem and positive school, peer, and family connections. Such programs focus on getting students involved in interactive, student-oriented, decision-making, cooperative learning activities, as well as including aspects of parental involvement, peer counseling, tutoring, and mentoring (McClean, 2002, p. 11).

Ultimately, there was a resounding consensus that mentored students' sense of family connectiveness improved after program completion, perhaps due to a carryover effect from students spending four months converging and developing positive relationships with an adult mentor. In addition, mentors encourage students to talk with their parents about the program and about any problems they were experiencing. The need to regularly communicate with parents was a message continually delivered to students and also an essential ingredient in peer mentoring.

At the same time, some mentoring programs have come under some criticism, which is not necessarily negative within a self but, in many venues, require some greater degree of insight as well as refinement. Mentor programs are proven effective in helping young imbibe moral values and eventually reduce the risk of their involvement in crime or violence. Mentoring is being more feasible than boot camps or being taken to adult courts. A mentor program called "Big Brothers/Big Sisters" provides volunteer services to children, including those from single-parent households. Another mentor program is "The Juvenile Mentoring Program," which has served more than 2,000 youths from twenty-five states.

Poor timing may be the benchmark of a bureaucratic system. In 1993, the Office of Juvenile Justice and Delinquency Prevention (OJJDP) proposed a "comprehensive strategy" for addressing the problem of juvenile crime. Under this comprehensive strategy, it was recognized that the family and the community, with support from other "core" social institutions, such as schools, churches, and local organizations, have primary responsibility for meeting the basic socializing needs of American children. It was recognized that failure to meet these basic needs is a primary contributor to juvenile crime. The author makes reference to the tarot or the stick approach: mentor program versus boot camps, waiver, and other punitive measures.

Unlike boot camps and waiver, mentor programs involve a helping, modeling strategy. Their most attractive feature is that rather than removing the youth from his environment, they take place in the community where the youth must learn to cope with his daily situations that significantly affect their lives. The mentoring relationship takes place in a dynamic setting that greatly increases the likelihood of success or failure. Most programs involve volunteer staff who see themselves as giving something to or sharing something with the youths who are being mentored.

Mentor programs are less costly than other approaches to delinquency prevention because often, the mentors are volunteers who may or may not receive reimbursement for out-of-pocket expenses relating to mentoring activities. In an ideal society concerned with the well-being of children, Cullen (1994) provides, perhaps, the best analytical approach for choosing the tarot (mentor) program over the sticks (boot camps and waiver). He suggests that social support rather than social control should be the primary focus for reducing rates of criminal involvement by youth in "high-risk neighborhoods" (Henriques, 1997, p. 8).

While mentoring reflects interconnectedness as perseverance in school as well as self-esteem, it also has been shown to reflect important values within other venues. Similarly, mentoring has proven to be highly positive for specific student demographic needs, such as students of color (in higher education). With the Higher Education Act of 1965, which allowed students to qualify for government financial aid, access to postsecondary education became a reality for many students of color who otherwise would not have had the opportunity to pursue a college degree. This "equal access" raised the hope of solving, through the benefits of a postsecondary education, the economic and social problems that people of color experience (Levin and Levin, 1991).

Education continues to be a major factor for upward mobility, and attainment of a bachelor's degree is the large, single factor responsible for the creation of the present black middle class. To this extent, the Adventor Program was introduced, utilizing proactive interventions and working with students. Key to the success of the Adventor Program is the relationship that develops between student and faculty member through the advising/mentoring relationship. The benefits derived from student-faculty interactions even outside of the classroom have been well documented. The positive benefits derived from these relationships are especially true for students of color. "Quality interaction with faculty seems to be more important than any other single college factor in determining minority student persistence" (Levin and Levin, 1991).

Combining the faculty advising relationship with a faculty mentoring relationship, as in the Adventor Program, creates a unique entity. Academic advising and mentoring programs are components of successful retention programs for students of color, especially the programs that are proactive and intrusive in nature. Successful advisement programs focus on academic, social, and emotional issues, goal clarification, and issues pertaining to student identification and connectiveness to the educational institution. Successful mentoring programs provide appropriate role models that encourage, help, and support students through the educational process, as well as help students deal with the intricacy of the institution they are attending.

Faculty involved with the Adventor Program balance their lives of advising and mentoring so that a unique nurturing and encouraging relationship develops. In the view of this author, this author should like to interject that the same thematic principles as identified in this topic are equally apropos. Adventor students receive the nurturing support they need while also being encouraged to take the risks required to become a scholar and lifelong learner. The Adventor Program relationship is designed so that it provides students with the skills necessary for success in a four-year university.

Adventor students develop increased feelings of self-esteem and self-worth. They receive academic and emotional support services that assist them in developing trust in their academic ability. Adventor students are better able to deal with peer rejection over academic involvement and to deal with any negative effects of racism and other forms of discrimination that they might experience on campus. The Adventor advisement/mentoring relationship is the vehicle for which Adventor students identify and become appropriately integrated into the academic and social cultures of the respective university (Coltin, 2001, p. 19).

It was concluded that the Adventor Program shows strong promise in retaining students of color. By implication, this would appear to reflect that such a collaborative program would have benefit for students of noncolor as well. By combining advising with mentoring in a proactive model, the college of education administration and faculty believe they have successfully made an impact on the higher attrition rates of students within the college of education.

As previously alluded to, peer mentoring has many benefits for many venues, including at-risk youth. In fact, mentoring programs for at risk-youth are growing at a rapid pace across the United States. Youth mentoring programs differ in their curriculum but most emphasize the relationship between a disadvantaged or troubled youngster and a caring adult. The relationship generally involves spending quality time together and providing support and guidance, with the aim of helping the young person better negotiate life's difficulties. To this, the literature on mentoring is mixed, and little research has adequately assessed the efficacy of mentoring programs.

The term *at-risk* is generally used to describe youth who come from single-parent homes who shows signs of emotional or behavioral problems and who lack the support to navigate developmental tasks successfully. As adults, they have a disproportionately high incidence of divorce, chronic unemployment, physical and psychiatric problems, substance abuse, demands on the welfare system, and further criminal activity (Paterson et al., 1989). The toll of these problems is costly, not only to the individual but also to society in terms of health care, welfare, and legal costs.

Once again, we witness the elements of mentoring programs as well as peer mentoring evidence themselves among these students and troubled teenagers. One organization, Big Brothers/Big Sisters, may be the best known volunteered mentoring program in the United States, matching at-risk youths with adult mentors. In one of the larger studies in the field (Tierney and Grossman, 1995), 959 youths who asked to be matched with a big brother/big sister during 1992-1993 were randomly assigned to one of two groups: a mentoring group or a control group. Both groups were interviewed when they applied for the program eighteen months later and completed self-report indices.

The study examined several broad areas that mentoring might affect: antisocial activities, academic performance, self-concepts, attitudes and behaviors, relationships with families, relationships with friends, and social and cultural enrichment, many of which have been identified by this author in the title of this literature review (section). The results indicated that "littles" (mentees) who met with their "bigs" (mentors) regularly for about a year were 46% less likely than the control group to start using illegal drugs, 27% less likely to start drinking, 52% less likely to skip a day of school, and 30% less likely to skip a class. In addition, the mentees were likely to be more trusting of their parents or guardians and less likely to lie to them, as well as to feel more supported and less criticized by their peers and friends. More than 70% of big-little matches at least three times a month for more than three hours at a time, and nearly half met once a week (Alessandri, 2002, p. 12).

Overall, the youth in this study were deemed to be "at risk" by a concerned professional who made a referral to the mentoring program. Similarly, at preintervention, mothers and teachers reported behavioral problems that placed these youths in the critical range for both internalizing and externalizing behaviors, confirming the at-risk territory. Cumulatively, self-reports indicated that the youths that were in the nonclinical range both before and after mentoring, which might qualify this group for mainstream academics students and suggest that either they did not see themselves as at risk or they were not honest about their feelings and behaviors. Regarding such questions about validity, only tentative conclusions were drawn by the authors.

Overall, mentoring (or peer mentoring) appears to be showing remarkable success throughout mainstream America's classrooms. HealthAmerica is the exclusive sponsor of the 2004 Big Brothers/ Big Sisters "Bigs in Schools" mentoring program in the Susquehanna school district. This school-based program pairs corporate volunteers and college and high schools students with elementary and middle schools students to form one-to-one mentoring relationships. Mentors meet the children at their schools at least three times each month.

Jan Hodges, executive vice president of HealthAmerica and Health Assurance, and Big Brothers/Big Sister's board member states, "After reviewing the Susquehanna Township School District's outcome evaluations for the 2000-2003 academic years, HealthAmerica enthusiastically committed to supporting this school-based mentoring program. The evaluations indicated that mentored children experienced significant improvements in academic performance; self-confidence; ability to express feelings; decision-making skills; sense of the future; attitudes towards school; relationships with peers; and relationships with other adults." These findings clearly illustrate the positive impact that a mentor and a role model can have on social, academic, and interpersonal development.

The Susquehanna Township School District currently has thirty-five elementary students matched with corporate and high school volunteers. HealthAmerica's fund will enable the school district to match an additional twenty to thirty children during the 2004 school year as well as help Big Brothers/Big Sisters recruit, screen, interview, and assess all prospective mentors for readiness and compatibility with the children. Again, this author feels that this has much to do with persistence. Individuals interested in volunteering must participate in a one—or two-day training session that provide in depth information on defining mentoring, setting realistic expectations, and communication. Additional training sessions are offered throughout the year.

Big Brothers/Big Sisters staff support and supervise mentors through monthly contact. At the end of the school year, mentors go through an exit interview and both teacher and mentors complete a program outcome evaluation (PR Newswire, 2004, p. 18). To a great extent, we once again witness the relationships of academic performance, persistence in school, and self-esteem in relationship to peer mentoring. These are common themes that are reflected throughout the literature and, in the view of this author, also comprise those successful ingredients that contribute to the impact of peer mentoring overall, not only throughout mainstream education but also with special needs populations.

As previously mentioned, peer mentoring often is understood by different names, some of which have already been referenced heretofore. Peer tutoring is another term that connotes important and essential understanding in conjunction with peer mentoring. To this extent, there represents a plethora of key studies. For example, at Crystal City High School, a program that pairs juniors and seniors with freshmen is having success with helping freshmen perform better in their classrooms, including peaceful, positive attitude in the school. The program is called mentoring. Juniors and seniors who choose to take part are assigned two or three freshmen to counsel, guide, and generally help with the transition into high school.

"There is something to be said about an older kid sitting with a younger kid talking to them about their problems and helping them. The big things we see here is a real camaraderie between the older kids and the younger kids," said Woody Gagnepain, Crystal City's counselor. Gagnepain said the program came from a similar effort in the 1980s. "We had some ideas about reaching students that we, as adults, weren't very successful getting through to," Gagnepain said. "We represent what teenagers dislike. We thought we would bridge the gap using their peers."

Gagnepain said that in the early 1990s, about 1,300 juniors and seniors worked with about the same amount of freshmen, mostly in tutoring, but the program wasn't very successful. He says the change came when the administrators let the mentoring take the form of more of a friendship. He said that this year 80 of the 120 juniors and seniors and only 3 or 4 of the 65 freshmen are not taking part in the program. "There is evidence enough to show that it works. Attendance has gone up, and our dropout rate is down. We have an extremely pleasant atmosphere. "We go months without conflicts or violence and we haven't seen a gun or a knife," Gagnepain said.

Gagnepain says the mentors go through two days of training through the National Council on Alcohol and Drug Abuse. He says a mentor can pull his or her freshman out of class at any time if there is a need to talk with the freshman or at the freshman's request. Then every three weeks, Gagnepain spends about two days with the teams of mentors to see how everyone is doing. He said the majority of the counseling by the mentors is on academic performance or social problems. "Sometimes they just want to sit and talk, and we make no apology about that because what they are doing is working," Gagnepain said. He added that if serious problems arose, the mentor could refer those problems to him.

Senior Robbie French, aged eighteen years, has been a mentor for the past two years. He says he has two freshmen with whom he works. "When I was a freshman, I had a mentor, and it was a really good experience, so I knew I wanted to do it," Robbie said. He spends about an hour each week in mentoring and meets with the two freshmen and Gagnepain every. He says the topic that is most addressed is schoolwork or academic performance. "We work on schoolwork, but we also become friends. Sometimes they want to talk about social issues and sometimes they need a little help relating to teachers. I had a tough case last year, but this year she is really doing well, so I like to think that I helped," Robbie said.

One of Robbie's freshmen is Matt Fields, aged fifteen years, who says that through his work with Robbie he has managed to get an A in a physical science class that was giving him trouble. He says that he was never intimidated by seniors the way some freshmen but having the help took some of the pressure off (Billingsly, 1998, p. 6). Herein, we see what appears to be an ideal example of peer mentoring. It was acknowledged that in the beginning, there was some trouble getting over the fear of being confident enough to talk to others, especially on the part of the mentees. Over time though and through communication, they were both able to overcome this problem together.

Similarly, while we witness important successes regarding the impact of peer mentoring as measured by academic performance, persistence in school, self-esteem, as well as a plethora of other items as have been identified, there exists a pervasive and fundamental concern for individuals with special needs or learning problems. Mentoring as an intervention for at-risk teens is becoming increasingly popular despite sparse evidence of its effectiveness. As part of the larger evaluation, reports on a four-year mentoring project developed specifically for African American adolescents, a study was undertaken.

Self-esteem, attitudes toward drugs and alcohol, grade, school attendance, and disciplinary infractions were examined using an experimental design. The most significant differences were found between the control and intervention groups. However, multiple explanations are offered to account why it is so difficult to document the positive benefits of mentoring among the population group in question. Although it has been noted that mentoring is increasingly viewed as an intervention for youth considered at risk, vulnerable, likely to be unprepared for adult living—at least according to some observers, while the overwhelming evidence is positive—this author should like to point out that as a way to fortify the inner-city youth against delinquency, school dropout, teen pregnancy, unemployment, and other negative life situations, formal matching of adult volunteers can be traced to the first Big Brothers Agency in 1902.

Despite this history, few empirical studies have documented the emphasis of mentoring on the lives of young people. Big Brothers/ Big Sisters, for example, have been providing adult support to youth from single-parent households for over 90, without evidence that "conclusively demonstrated that youth who participated in Big Brothers/Big Sisters programs fared better than they would have had they not participated. While Big Brothers/Big Sisters have begun a four year research initiative, the most recent report on the project stated, "It remains to be seen whether developmental mentoring relationships can produce real changes in the lives of youth, such as improved grades and more positive behavior."

Silcker and Palmer (1993) have also observed a "clear lack of research on the effects of a mentoring relationship with low achievement high school dropouts" (Royse, 1998, p. 5). The literature suggests an explanation as to why mentoring programs have produced mixed results. Hamilton and Hamilton (1992) observed that mentors often have different views of their purpose. What they call level 1 mentors saw their primary purpose as developing relationship. Level 2 mentors spoke about introducing options as their major purpose. Level 3 mentors stress developing character, while level 4 mentors focused on developing competence. Mentors who viewed their purpose as relationship building worried about whether they were liked and if they had chosen the right activities.

According to the author, Hamilton and Hamilton concluded that an emphasis on learning to do something produced the most functional pairs. In some, few objective data exist on the effects of mentoring programs on adolescents. The purpose of the research in question as cited is to report on an outcome evaluation of a locally developed mentoring program that targeted African American teens.

Chapter III:
Methods

Throughout this section, this author shall hone in on different types of research methods that this author may be utilizing, albeit not exclusive to one. As this is a qualitative study, this author believes that the most effective and salient methods include conflict resolution, peer mediation, and peer mentoring. Of course, there are others, and this author is also of the belief that depending upon the respective school or setting, some elements from different strategies may be used in tandem with one another, while peer mentoring may prove to be the most effective of all—all left up to the discretion of the teacher, who after all, maintains a hands-on understanding of the immediate problem.

However, these many strategies, as alluded to, can be quite useful in preventing violent and disruptive behavior that runs counter to education throughout our country's schools, with particular emphasis upon the aforementioned age group or for purposes of this dissertation, this author shall refer to them for the most part throughout this dissertation as the early adolescent years, which allows for some degree of latitude throughout high schools, middle schools, and even elementary schools. Indeed, it is a serious problem not only for the overall objective of education, but also for the impact it has on teachers.

As a kind of preface to some of those more effective strategies, that is, conflict resolution, many problems/solutions begin at a young age in school. With this in mind, this author should like to let this be the basis for subsequent discussion and analysis, especially regarding aggressive behavior in the classroom as well as effective strategies that can prevent and curtail the same. This author believes that the prevention or the curtailing of the problem includes many, that is, teachers, social workers, school counselors, administrators, parents, and even the co-opting of other schools (and teachers) as well as the community.

One author outlines social and psychological risk factors related to violence in schools and described strategies and programs that bring families and schools together to prevent future violence. Similarly, the author identifies specific risk factors that double the probability that the youth will commit a violent act as delineated in the review of literature section. What is particularly troubling to this author, particularly in the area of educating and education, is that studies show that poor school performance and absenteeism (a very serious problem and, to an extent, much underrated) is strongly associated with peer rejection, especially in early childhood.

Another risk factor related to school violence is being a victim of school bullying or feeling rejected or disrespected. This author has paid much attention to the problem of *bullying,* as it is the belief of this author that bullying is a grossly underrated and not attended reality that can virtually disrupt an individual's entire life, both in school and out of school. Furthermore, it can be the prime or sole cause of bad grades, psychological problems, and failure.

According to Boulter (2004) violence prevention is dependent upon family-school connection and family involvement in the school. Effective school-based strategies and programs that prevent future violence emphasize the importance of building strong parent, school, and community partnership. Schools and parents together can successfully replace violence and aggressive behavior by teaching, modeling, and reinforcing pro-social behavior, such as altruism and empathy, plus effective coping and problem-solving strategies to deal with frustration and anger. Of course, this relates primarily to bullying, but and as this author has previously indicated, many of these strategies are interrelating and teachers may pluck those "nuggets" or most useful aspects of the varying strategies to best compliment their individual type of aggressive behavior within their particular schools.

At this time, however, this author should like to focus upon conflict resolution as an essential strategy, mainly because it is arguably the most successfully and pervasively used strategies in America's schools. Similarly, peer mediation as well as peer mentoring should also be considered in tandem with conflict resolution. There exists much "gold to be mined" in the form of human resources (HR) that may emanate from upper classmen.

Very often, high school seniors (especially), and perhaps juniors, being older, do respond to responsibility. When identified and chosen correctly, these attributes may be channeled toward curtailing aggressive behavior, including bullying and a host of other forms of aggressive behavior as delineated within this Review of Literature section. As previously indicated, this author should like to address and discuss conflict resolution as well as peer mediation and peer mentoring in tandem, as it is the belief of this author that the three, exclusive of the last, reflect similar underlying tenets that have already proven to be highly effective throughout America's schools. Indeed, aggressive behavior can take many forms.

While at the outset of this (Review of Literature) section, this author made reference to conflict resolution and the fact that many schools have adopted their own "brand" of conflict resolution and implemented the same within the classroom setting. Indeed, many schools have experienced positive and successful results with conflict resolution in school, as this author finds to be of such paramount importance.

Similarly and concurrent with conflict resolution are both peer mediation and peer mentoring programs. For example and as reported by Dounic et al., effective school-wide responses to disruptive, aggressive, and violent student behaviors are critical to ensuring teacher and student safety and to increasing constructive approaches to conflict. As such, many educators are implementing school-based prevention programs focused on conflict resolution and peer mediation (CR/PM).

As disruptive, aggressive, violent behaviors appear to be more prevalent throughout the school population, schoolwide approaches to discipline are critical to ensuring safety and increasing appropriate student-school interaction. Classroom teachers often have available options when faced with disruptive or aggressive actions. In addition, administrative decisions in dealing with inappropriate behavior are frequently punitive, resulting in student suspension from school or in placement in alternative school settings, yet few professionals would agree that punitive actions to disruptive, violent, or aggressive acts teach appropriate behavior or are effective in the long term. As previously indicated, a harder hand was taken during the 1980s and 1990s, with armed guards, metal detectors, and the like, which has given way to less-heavy-handed or punitive types of approaches.

Conflict resolution programs typically include a curriculum designed to teach students to acknowledge individuals differences, change win-lose paradigms to win-win solutions, and use negotiations to resolve conflicts. Interventions based on conflict resolution may also include specific information on mediation of conflict by typically trained peers. Peer mediation is a structured conflict consistent of specific steps to help disputants define and solve a problem and move away from dependence on punitive, seclusionary methods. It includes an attempt to affect how students conceptualize conflict.

As previously identified (i.e., Review of Literature section), proponents suggest that an effective PM method can do the following: (1) provide students with a framework for solving conflicts; (2) give students and opportunity to assume responsibility for their own behavior; (3) lower teacher stress by reducing the number of student conflicts they have to handle; (4) increase instruction on hand; and (4) help students understand how cultural diversity can affect interpersonal communication and human interaction.

Over the past recent years, authors have investigated the effectiveness of a schoolwide CR curriculum and PM program. Working in three middle schools in the US Southeast, the authors specifically examined the protocols necessary to implementing a successful media program, factors that facilitated its effectiveness, and the way students learned to manage their peer conflicts. The conceptual underpinnings of CR/

PM programs are rooted in developmental and sociopsychological theories.

Students entering adolescence have increasing dependence and identity needs. Those who develop positive and adequate mechanisms for coping with the complex demands of their environment have an excellent chance of growing into emotionally healthy adults. This further helps to fulfill the school as a place of learning as well as preparing young adults for their post-education experience or, to put it another way, productive citizens. Successful coping requires acquisition of new approaches to challenging situations when outmoded responses stop working.

Chapter IV:
Findings

Ultimately, while this author has identified the qualitative solution to reducing aggressive behavior and resolving conflicts in schools, this author should further like to hone in upon those most effective solutions designed to reduce aggressive behavior and resolve conflicts in schools. As previously mentioned, these would fall largely within the scope of conflict resolution, and it may also fairly be characterized (i.e., conflict resolution (CR)) as incorporating both peer mediation and peer mentoring. As previously alluded to, some reports have indicated that little is known about the effectiveness of implementing CR/PM training, while others seem to be quite seasoned in this area and have long since gone on to higher successful implementation project, as is the case throughout hundreds, if not thousands, of schools throughout the United States as of this writing.

At this point, this author should like to pause enough to state that this very factor, that is, CR/PM, despite the very fact that it has stood head and shoulders above many other techniques aimed at reducing aggressive behavior in the schools, seems, to this author, to underscore a much greater need for co-opting among teachers, schools, school districts, and others. Similarly, available data suggest that some projects may modify youths' self-reported attitudes about violent behavior, improve school discipline, and reduce absenteeism (in the view of this author, arguably among the worst offenders or aspects of overall aggressive behavior).

More attention needs to be paid to evaluating CR/PM projects. Some data suggest they that may contribute positively to community efforts to reduce violence among youths, but insufficient information exists to know what project best serves which students and how a project should be implemented. It is for this reason that, as this author has previously stated, whatever strategy a teacher chooses—and they may well be parts of varied strategies, that is, conflict resolution, peer mediation, peer mentoring—would go a long way in filling this void.

Finally, regarding the findings of this qualitative analysis, this author would iterate the most powerful/proven techniques, for example, conflict resolution, peer mediation, and peer mentoring. In conclusion, this author should like to focus more on peer mentoring, which in the view of this author, has so much in common with both conflict resolution and peer mediation. As this author has made reference to both conflict resolution (CM) and peer mediation (PM), this author has discussed both in tandem, while in point of fact they are technically not the same as per this author's previously stated definition(s).

Consequently and at this juncture, this author should like to address peer mediation in greater detail. This shall also address peer mentoring, especially given its "proximity" to "peer mediation" as measured by academic performance, persistence in school, self-esteem, as well as those dynamics that appear relevant, as well as pervasive throughout the literature, especially experimental studies. Peer mentoring means different things to different people, while for the central purpose of the findings, this author is particularly interested with the students helping students, while important benefits have been found among co-teaching and educators mentoring students.

The mentoring relationship between faculty staff/ staff mentors and college students' protégées was examined to identify differences in how each participant evaluated their relationship. Questioning data from 205 faculty staff/staff mentor and 122 school protégées were analyzed. While students were more positive than their mentors in addressing the overall value of mentoring relationship, they were relatively unaware that mentors might enter into the relationship to obtain benefits to the mentors. Assessments of mentoring were unrelated to gender or status of either mentor or protégée.

The research mentoring in education settings ranges broadly from peer mentoring in secondary education to studies of faculty/ graduate mentoring in doctoral programs. According to Freuke and Dahlgren (1996), the mentoring itself takes on a variety of forms. In some cases, formal programs are administered in which students are assigned to mentors. The program has proven to be highly successful and accomplishes the following objectives through several university-wide efforts:

1. peer mentoring
2. mandatory student orientation course within each academic college
3. new student assessment
4. advising programs

Program activities encourage high academic performance, responsible citizenship, and culture sensitivity. Overall, it is the belief that co-mentoring, especially as relates to academic performance, is increasingly understood in a number of variables, which to a large extent and in the view of this author, are best understood in terms of culture and context, size of institution, values, lack of student involvement, strategies for building and maintaining communities, increasing access and diversity, expanding leadership opportunities, and developing effective retention programs.

Integrating curricula has received positive results, as has peer mentoring, giving individuals (students) a greater reason to succeed, especially among their peers, and the sense of increased accountability serves to advance the very concept that is peer mentoring. Ultimately, this author is primarily concerned with the impact of peer mentoring as well as conflict resolution and peer mediations as measured by academic performance, persistence in school, and self-esteem.

References

Alessandri, Michael. (2002, December 22). *The affects of a monitoring program on at risk youth. Adolescents.*

Billingsly, Linda M. (1998, December 14). *Mentoring program helps Crystal City freshmen upperclassmen provide guidance to schools newcomers. St. Louis Post Dispatch.*

Boulter, Lyn. (January 1, 2004). Family School Connection and School Violence Prevention. *Negro Educational review.*

Brinson, Jessie, A. (June 22, 1994). Cross Cultural Conflict Resolution in the Schools: *Some Practical Intervention Strategies from Counselors. Journal of Counseling and Development.*

Campbell, Toni A. (2000, December 1). *The mentoring relationship: different perceptions of benefits. College Student Journal.*

Chattopadhyay, Sajal. (August 24, 2007). *The Effectiveness of Universal School Based Programs for the Prevention of Violent and Aggressive Behavior: A Report on Recommendations of a Task Force on Community Preventive Services. Morbidity and Mortality Weekly Report.*

Chory-Assad, Rebecca M.; Cicchirillo, Vincent. (December 1, 2005). *Effects of Affective Orientation and Video Game Play on Aggressive*

Thoughts and Behaviors. Journal of Broadcasting and Electronic Media.

Colton, Cynthia. (2001, September 22). *The Adventor Program: advisors and mentoring for students of color in higher education. Journal of Humanistic Counseling, Education and Development.*

Daunic, Ann P. et al. (November 1, 2000). School-wide Conflict Resolution and Peer Mediation Programs: Experiences in three Middle Schools. *Intervention School and Clinics.*

Myburgh, Cph. (December 22, 2005). *The Phenomenon of Aggressive Behavior of Learners in the School Situation. Education.*

Gannon, Jeanette et al. (October 1, 1998). *A Decreasing Violent or Aggressive theme play among pre-school Children with Behavior Disorders. Exceptional Children.*

Greer-Chase, Marlene et al. (May 1, 2002). *Why the Prevention of Aggressive Disruptive Behavior in Middle School must begin in Elementary School. The Clearing House.*

Halasyamani, Lakshmi et al., (December 1, 1995), *A Review of Selected School-Based Conflict Resolution and Peer Mediation projects, Journal of School Health*

Henriques, Zelma Weston. (1997, December 22). *Promises and pitfalls of mentoring as a juvenile justice strategy. Social Justice.*

Makkai, Toni. (2004, March 1). *Sports, physical activity and anti-social behavior in youth. Youth Studies Australia.*

Manns, Derrick. (2001, June 22). *Maintaining students' sense of community in a multiversity. Academic Exchange Quarterly.*

McClean, Warren. (2002, September 1). *Increasing self esteem and school connectiveness through a multidimensional mentoring program. Journal of School Health.*

PR Newswire. (2004, March 18). *HealthAmerica and Health Assurance fund school based mentoring program: working conjunction with Big Brothers/Big Sisters of the capital region.*

Royse, David. (1998, March 22). *Mentoring high risk minorities: evaluation of the Brothers' project. Adolescents*

Smith, Darla R. (2004, January 1). *Integrating physical education, math and physics. The Journal of Physical, Recreation and Dance.*

Thomas, Sandra T., (January 1, 2003), *Handling Anger in the Teacher-Student Relationship, Nation Education Perspectives,* p. 11

Van Acker, Richard, (January 1, 2007), *Antisocial, Aggressive, and Violent Behavior in Children and Adolescents Within Alternative Education Settings: Prevention and Intervention, Preventing School Failure,* p. 9